BEING PRESENT

to God | to self | to others

by Pastor Mark Borseth

To purchase additional copies of Being Present: to God, to Self, to Others, use this QR code:

ISBN 979-8-9897154-9-7 (paperback)

Library of Congress Control Number: 2024918757

Email: Prmark@rlcok.org

Cataloging info:

RELIGION/Christian Living/Devotional
RELIGION/Christian Living/Inspirational
RELIGION/ Christian Living/Spiritual Growth

This book is dedicated to all those who have helped me learn that experiencing God happens best in the context of Christian community and just as often (if not more) outside the walls of the church as within them.

I want to especially thank my family. Thanks Betsy, Nathan, Andrew and Peter for all the sacrifices you have made to support me when the demands of ministry left me with less to offer you than you deserved. As I discover that the best way to encounter God is through relationships and through loving and serving others, I hope that makes me better and more in intentional in my investment in you.

Next, I want to thank the congregation of Resurrection Lutheran Church in Yukon, Oklahoma for allowing me to be led by the Holy Spirit in my ministry and giving me a sabbatical to more intentionally focus on experiencing God through unity in the community.

Finally, I want thank my ministry colleagues in Yukon for your friendship and encouragement. It has only been through experiencing more of God through knowing you that I have learned the true value of Christian unity.

MARK BORSETH

table of contents

table of contents, continued

FOREWORD

In John 17, Jesus gives us a strategy for fulfilling the Great Commission: our love for one another is how the people around us come to know who Jesus is and how much God loves them. In this book, Mark employs a rhythm to help us be an answer to Jesus' John 17 prayer.

Being present to self, God, and others are necessary precursors to unity and community. The evaluation tools, the practical applications, and the Biblical insights all combine to powerfully align us with Jesus' own heartbeat.

But while it's a quick read, don't read it quickly!

Savor and reflect on each day's devotional as it's designed and you will be glad you did.

Pastor Dave Drum
Executive Director, J17 Ministries

BEING PRESENT

to God | to self | to others

by Pastor Mark Borseth

INTRODUCTION

When you are in love, you take full advantage of every opportunity to be with that person, using any and every excuse to be together. Jesus desires His followers to take advantage of every opportunity to be with Him.

We are often quite faithful at spending time with him in private prayer, study, and worship. But there are other places Jesus says He will be waiting for us. If we simply make a point to be where He says He will be.

1

WHERE JESUS SAYS HE WILL BE

Many of us are in the habit of meeting with Jesus during prayer, Bible study, Sunday worship. But he is also waiting to meet us in other places as well. Two of those places are

- when we gather in unity with other Christians and
- when we live out our faith in service to the neighbors in our community.

Jesus says, unambiguously, He will be with us when we gather with other Christians in His name. In Matthew 18:20, He says,

> "For where two or three are gathered in my name, I am there among them."

If Jesus, our beloved, is going to be where there is unity among Christians, how can we more intentionally seek out such unity, affording us more time to spend with him?

Jesus also promises to be with us as we love and serve others throughout our daily lives. In Matthew 25 Jesus says when we serve "the least of these" we are really serving Him. Then, in Matthew 28, Jesus tells his disciples that as they go and make disciples of others He will be with them. If Jesus is going to be where we daily live our faith, as we love and serve others, perhaps we should become more intentional in seeing, loving, and serving the people God places along our path.

If our private, formal times of connection are the only places we encounter Jesus, we are missing out on so many ways to fellowship with our Savior. Let's look a little deeper at how Jesus wants to meet with us when we intentionally seek lives of unity within our community.

Rendezvous Point #1 Unity with other Christians

Jesus promises to be present with us as we gather with other Christians in His name. That is a great blessing to us, but it is also meant to bless others. Jesus says that our unity will bless others as they get a clearer picture of who He is when we are unified.

The context of the entire eighteenth chapter of Matthew is about relationships with other believers. The chapter begins with the way children are treated. The way we honor and bless children affects the level and quality of our connection with God. If we dishonor children, or cause them to stumble in faith, we cut ourselves off from experiencing God. Jesus then goes on to talk about a good shepherd who is willing to leave the ninety-nine to restore the one lost sheep back to the community. Next, He talks about an intentional strategy for healing divisions in the church. It is only then, after all this talk about relationships and unity, that Jesus says when people gather in His name, He will be with them.

As we continue to read Matthew 18, Jesus tells Peter to not set limits on forgiving others and illustrates his point by telling the story of an unforgiving servant. Because he is unwilling to forgive others, he is separated from his own relationship with the master who has forgiven him his great debt. Unity and reconciled relationships are vitally important to more powerfully experiencing Jesus. A direct connection exists between the unity we have with members of the body of Christ and our ability to experience Jesus' presence.

Our unity with other Christians is not just to benefit us as individuals or as a Christian community. It allows others to witness what God is like. In John 17, Jesus prays that His followers will have the same unity with each other that He has with the Father. He says that when *that kind of unity* happens,

> ***... "then the world will know that you (Father) sent me and have loved them even as you have loved me."*** (John 17:23)

Jesus also tells his disciples at the last supper that the way they love each other will reveal to unbelievers what it looks like to be his disciple.

> ***"By this everyone will know that you are my disciples, if you love one another."*** (John 13:35)

In summary, as we have unity with other believers, we will experience the presence of Jesus more fully. And, others will want what we have. But, if we foster disunity and division, the opposite will happen. We will not experience Jesus' presence individually or as a community. Even worse, we will more likely cause people to *turn away* from Jesus than turn towards Him.

Rendezvous Point #2 Living Our Faith in the Community

Jesus tells us we will also encounter Him as we go out and minister to those who don't yet know Him. When Jesus was about to ascend to the Father, He told His disciples they would not lose contact with Him, but would continue to encounter Him in different ways. He says in Matthew 28:19-20,

> ***"Therefore go and make disciples of all nations, baptizing them in the name of the Father and of the Son and of the Holy Spirit, 20 and teaching them to obey everything I have commanded you. And surely I am with you always, to the very end of the age."*** Matthew

28:19-20 New International Version 19

We are included in that commission.

And we have the same promise that as we go, He will be with us.

In Matthew 25, Jesus encourages his disciples to stay awake so they will not miss out on encountering Him in the places He will be. He begins with the Parable of the Foolish Virgins who don't have oil in their lamps and miss out when the bridegroom comes unexpectedly. Then, He continues with the Parable of the Talents, where those who invest what they have been given to honor the master and bless others enter into the joy of the master. But the one who buries his talent and keeps it to himself misses out. Finally, Matthew 25 concludes with what is often referred to as the Parable of the Sheep and the Goats. It tells how His followers who didn't go into the community and care for their neighbors in need regularly missed out on his Presence. Those who did go and serve their neighbors regularly encountered Him.

> ***"Truly I tell you, just as you did it to one of the least of these who are members of my family, you did it to me."***
> Matthew 25:40 NIV

When we go out into the community and love and serve our neighbors, we will encounter *more* than just our neighbors. We will encounter Jesus as well.

Another way we encounter the presence of God in our daily lives is to use the gifts of the Holy Spirit to love and serve others. These gifts are given to us by God to not only be used inside the church building, but wherever we go. Some of the greatest healings, most powerful prophetic words, and most profound experiences of God's presence, happen in the community as we allow the Holy Spirit to lead us in seeing, in loving, and in serving our neighbors.

We needlessly starve ourselves of opportunities to encounter Jesus. When we keep our relationship with Jesus private—private prayer, private devotions, private worship—we rob ourselves of moments when the power of the Holy Spirit can work in and through us. We need to be intentional in seeking out those times and places of encounter: *times of unity with other Christians* and being led by the Spirit *to love and serve the people in our community*. Our most powerful encounters with Jesus may not happen in the church building. They may be at work, at school, walking in our neighborhood, or maybe standing in line at Walmart!

2

BEING FULLY PRESENT

As we focus on being where Jesus is, the next challenge is learning to be fully present when we are in those places—present to ourselves, present to God, and present to the people who are right in front of us. It does little good to be where Jesus says He will be if, when we are there, we are *not truly present*.

Sometimes, we can be physically present with the ones we love, but not really there. We may be tired from a hard day's work. We may be depressed about things that haven't happened in the way we hoped. We may be anxious about what might happen tomorrow. We may be thinking about what we need to do when we get home again or back to work. We may be in bondage to addiction or depression, both of which rob us of even being able to be present in the moment.

Just as we can physically be with the people in our life, but not really be present, we can have the same thing happen in our relationship with Jesus. We can be in the right places—Christian unity and serving others in the community—but not really be present. Even if we are physically in the right place, we can still miss out on what God wants us to experience if we are not fully present.

I have seen this in my own life. Exhaustion, depression, and anxiety have often decreased my capacity to be fully present and available to the ones I love. At a young age I learned to medicate my emotions with addictive behavior which limited my ability to be present in the moment. I was in the right place at the right time, but was not really present, experiencing connections and intimacy.

I admit, I have struggled with being truly present to myself, to God, and to the person in front of me. What about you? In which of these three areas do you need to improve to more fully experience Jesus?

I. Being Present to Self

We can be in all the right places at all the right times and still miss out on what God wants us to experience. I grew up in a stoic Norwegian family in Iowa where my dad had PTSD from the Korean War. My mom was schizophrenic. That atmosphere led me to have some significant deficiencies processing emotions and connecting with others. I struggled daily with those challenges. They affected the depth of my relationships with myself, God, and others. I often felt like an outsider looking in.

Because of my issues with connection, I found myself uncomfortable in my own emotions. Especially the negative ones. Instead of learning to manage those emotions in healthy and productive ways, I often escaped into fantasy, or found whatever drug I could access to medicate my discomfort—food, pornography, good grades, awards at school. Because of my inability to be present to myself, I often failed to experience what was right in front of me. It was difficult to be present to God or to others as well.

How many of us go to church every week, read the Bible, and try to live good Christian lives but never really experience God because we're afraid to be present to ourselves? Our addictions destroy the connection with self, which in turn destroys our relationship with God and others. Busyness and exhaustion allow us to never really live in the present, therefore avoiding God and others. Shame and guilt keep us stuck in the past, while anxiety and fear keep us fixated on the future. All of these hinder us from being fully present.

Jesus' invitation to be present in Christian unity and community requires us to be more than just physically present. He desires for us to be emotionally and spiritually present as well—not just going through the motions, pretending to connect, observing from the outside.

If you choose to accept this challenge to be fully present where Jesus is, the place to start is an honest evaluation.

Are able to be to be present with yourself?

During this challenge, be prepared to let God heal and grow your ability to be present to yourself, to let go of the shame and mistakes of the past and no longer let them prevent you from living in the present.

•This is the time to trust God with your future and fully live in the now.

•This is the time to slow down and rest, so you can be present to the people and situations of life.

•This is the time to address physical and emotional problems which hinder your ability to be present.

•This is the time to begin the healing process for any addiction which has kept you from being able to be present to yourself, to God, and to the people in your life.

II. Being Present to God

If you are unable to be present to yourself, you will probably not be able to experience God's presence very well either. Even if you are present to yourself, it is possible, even easy, to live without being present to, or aware of, God. Our society actually encourages us to live life without God and live solely for our own benefit.

In seventeenth century France, a monk named Brother Lawrence drew the attention of people from around Europe. Though he was a simple kitchen worker, he experienced God while washing dishes and floors in ways that priests and bishops were unable to duplicate even in their well-performed rituals. Because of how Brother Lawrence intentionally practiced the presence of God, he lived a life that looked very different from even the greatest leaders of the church.

Today, it is not uncommon for people who identify as Christians to have very little conscious awareness of God throughout the day. They may serve on church committees, work on church service projects, attend Bible studies and worship services, and yet not sense any personal connection with God during these activities.

Some may have grown up in, or been influenced by, an arm of the church that downplays the personal experience of God, or even teaches that God is not active in the world today. So why would they have any expectation of encountering God's presence and power in their daily life?

For others, it is not that they don't believe God wants to have a connection with them. They have simply never learned how to hear God's voice through scripture reading or had any expectation to hear from God in their prayer life. Instead, Bible study is for information rather than relationship, and prayer is a one-way monolog to God, rather than a dialog with God.

If you decide to take this challenge to be fully present where Jesus is, it might be time to look at your theology.

•Do you believe God still speaks to his followers?

•Do you expect the Holy Spirit to live in you and work through you?

•Do you expect God to speak to you through the scriptures or do you just read the Bible to learn information?

•Do you expect to hear God when you pray?

•Do you journal conversations with God?

•Do you practice God's presence in your daily life and not just at church on Sunday?

This is your time to become consciously aware of God, be present to hear His voice, and to be led daily by his Holy Spirit. Not just for an hour on Sunday, but 24/7.

III. Being Present to the Person in Front of Us

It is possible to be present to ourselves and present to the reality that God is with us, but still not be present to the people around us. When Christianity becomes only about how God can bless us personally, and we don't allow that relationship with God to lead us into loving and serving our neighbors, our ability to fully experience God will most certainly be stunted.

In the *Parable of the Good Samaritan* (Luke 10:25-37), Jesus shows his followers how easy it is to think we are good servants of God yet be so focused on our personal agenda that we fail to love and serve our neighbor. We often narrow our definition of who our neighbor is, allowing us to ignore certain people or groups rather than choose to be a neighbor to whomever we encounter.

In the *Parable of the Sheep and Goats* (Matthew 25:31-46), Jesus reveals how we can believe we are good members of the body of Christ yet never leave the comfort zone of living for ourselves. He shares how seeing, loving, and serving our neighbor in need is how we encounter His presence.

•What if Peter and John had not seen and ministered to the lame man at the gate of the temple (Acts 3)?

•What if Philip hadn't gone out to the wilderness road where he encountered the Ethiopian eunuch (Acts 8)?

•What if Jesus hadn't encountered the woman at the well (John 4), or Zacchaeus in the sycamore tree (Luke 19)?

•What if Ananias had not listened to God and not ministered to Saul in Damascus (Acts 9)?

Many of our encounters with God are contingent on whether we allow Him to lead us out of ourselves and into connection with others. If you take this challenge to be fully present where Jesus is, it will mean turning from self and intentionally toward the needs of others. Possibly even toward those you would never have chosen to engage with. It will probably mean stopping for a person in need, rather than walking by.

All of this sounds good, you say. But is there any evidence these things will make a difference in my life?

In the next chapter you will hear stories from the ministry of Jesus, the early church, and throughout the last 2,000 years of church history. You will see what a difference it makes when people are fully present to self, to God, and to others, seeking out the places Jesus says He will be.

Our journey so far has led us from being where Jesus says He will be as we connect with other believers to being where Jesus says He will be as we connect with others within our community. When we understand the importance of being fully present to self, to God, and to the person in front of us, we will be where Jesus says He will be—***connecting with other believers*** and ***connecting with others within our community***.

3

UNITY IN THE COMMUNITY

If we are going to live a life built around how Jesus related to his followers, we should learn more about Jesus' ministry to his disciples. According to Mark 3:14, Jesus began his ministry by choosing his disciples to do two things:

- be with Him in unity and
- be sent by Him into the community

During the three years of His earthly ministry, Jesus gathered his disciples together and lived in unity with them. Then He sent them out in pairs to proclaim and demonstrate the Kingdom of God in the community.

After his resurrection, Jesus gathered them together and sent them out into the world just as the Father had sent Him (John 20:21). Then, when He was about to ascend, He gathered his disciples on a mountain and sent them out to make disciples of all nations (Matthew 28:16-20).

After his ascension, 120 of his followers gathered in unity for ten days to pray. And as they did, the Holy Spirit came upon them to send them out into the streets to be His witnesses, first in Jerusalem, then in Judea, then in Samaria, then to the ends of the earth.

The Apostle Paul did the same. He gathered believers in large meetings and house to house, followed by countless journeys into the community and beyond to witness about Jesus.

Do you feel the rhythm?

Coming together and being sent should be the normal practice for Jesus' followers. Not just 2,000 years ago, but now as well. Encountering Jesus and the gifts of the Holy Spirit inside the church walls is a given in the life of a Christian. Yes, there will still be private times of prayer and study and worship. But the rhythm of every believer's life should include regularly coming together in Christian unity to meet Jesus and encounter the Holy Spirit then regularly going out to live our faith in the community.

Throughout history, groups who learned this rhythm of being together and being sent have had the greatest impact on their communities, nations, and the world.

Here are a few examples:

The Moravians

The Moravians were a group of mostly refugees, fleeing religious persecution in what is now the Czech Republic. They found a new home in Germany on the estate of Nicholas Zinzendorf, a Lutheran Count.

Nicholas Zinzendorf grew up in a pietistic family, regularly hearing stories from people living out their faith in the world. While visiting an art gallery in Dusseldorf, he had a mystical encounter and sensed a call from God. He joined a group called the Order of the Mustard seed, which eventually grew and spread around the world. The members were to commit to, and take on, the following rules for life:

•True to Christ
•Kind to people
•Take the gospel to the nations

The identifying mark of its members was a ring with the inscription "None of us lives for himself". They wore the ring to remind themselves to live according to the rules of the order.

Because of his commitment as part of this group, Zinzendorf knew he must offer hospitality to the refugees. This community grew and all was well until the growing diversity of the group led to division. By the summer of 1727, the religious refugees living on Zinzendorf's estate were experiencing significant disunity. Zinzendorf went door to door, urging unity and reconciliation among the group. On August 13 the community gathered at the Lutheran Church in Berthelsdorf for a Communion service, and the Holy Spirit was present in a powerful way. The presence of God was so tangible, those at the service testified they didn't know if they were in heaven or still on earth!

The effects of this encounter went far beyond that one worship service. Those who were there and experienced God's Presence:

•Began small group ministries where people could share life together, pray with each other, and hold each other accountable.
•Began a 24/7 prayer movement which would last for over 100 years.
•Sent missionaries around the world (this number equaled those sent by the rest of the Protestants in Europe combined)

The Moravians were willing to work with any Christian group without taking any credit for themselves. They worked with, and blessed, various other denominations. Such ecumenism was very rare in their day. Even today, their brand name "Moravian" is not nearly as well known as the work they do around the world.

Several of their missionaries encountered a discouraged young man named John Wesley. Wesley saw in the Moravians a depth of faith and experience of God he knew he lacked in himself. So he joined with them as they gathered for worship and prayer in London. At one of those meetings at Aldersgate he felt his heart strangely warmed. Then, at another of those gatherings, the Holy Spirit showed up in such a powerful way Wesley was transformed. This led to birth of Methodism. Methodism took from the Moravians their focus on gathering in unity to be sent out into the community (and around the world) and would become a large part of the impetus behind the First Great Awakening.

Azusa Street

With the turn of the 20th century, many diverse Christian groups hungered for an outpouring of the Holy Spirit. In Topeka, Kansas, Charles Parham formed a ministry school focused on restoring the church to its roots in the book of Acts. He would later start a school in Houston, Texas where one of the students was William Seymour, the son of former slaves. Because of his skin color, Seymour had to listen from the hallway. But Parham kept the door open to make sure he could hear. Seymour was so affected by what was happening in Parham's school he initiated an interracial prayer meeting at Azusa Street in Los Angeles. In 1906, a diverse group of people, men, women, young, old, black, white, Latino, all sitting next to each other in worship, was quite unique.

As they gathered in unity the Holy Spirit was present in powerful ways. Many encountered the Holy Spirit not just when they got to the meetings, but even on the way there. Testimonies of these encounters spread back to the homes of the attendees and then all around the world. Pentecostal writer and evangelist Frank Bartelman said of Azusa: *"...the color line was erased by the blood of Jesus."*

The combination of unity and a hunger to experience the presence of God fanned the flame of evangelism which would burn like wildfire into the greatest missionary movement in world history, spreading the gospel of Jesus Christ throughout the world.

Alcoholics Anonymous, WW2 and Beyond

In the early 20th century, God got the attention of a Lutheran Pastor from Pennsylvania named Frank Buchman. Buchman was feeling deep resentment toward ministry partners he thought had wronged him. He discovered his resentment got in the way of his ability have healthy connections with himself, others, and with God. In 1921 he started what was called The Oxford Society which taught that fear, selfishness, and lack of contact with God were the root causes of many of society's problems.

As a remedy, Buchman formed communities of people committed to:

- absolute honesty
- absolute purity

- absolute selflessness
- absolute love

These absolutes were to be combined with a commitment to seek daily contact with God.

Some of the early attendees of these groups discovered when they lived in community, according to these principles, they experienced the unexpected side effect of delivery from alcoholism.The amazing thing—the ones experiencing this freedom had been written off as lost causes by medical and psychiatric professionals. This type of group led to the beginnings of Alcoholics Anonymous and eventually led to several other 12-step programs addressing other addictions.

These pioneers of Alcoholics Anonymous discovered that coming from a life of shame and isolation into a community where they could be fully present to themselves, to each other, and to God led to a spiritual awakening. It inspired them to go and share what they had experienced with others having the same struggles.

But Buchman's influence on world history did not end there. His conviction that people who lived according to the Four Absolutes, while seeking regular conscious contact with God, was exactly what the world needed--especially during the years of growing Fascism, Communism, and the spread of wars around the world. In 1938 he formed a group called Moral Rearmament. He believed that people resorted to Fascism and Communism to find a way to make the world make sense and saw many walk away from Fascism and Communism once they experienced what he had to offer. His impact would touch every part of the world, from South America to Europe to India to China. His efforts were officially recognized after WW2 by the nations of Germany and France as being the reason the two countries were able to achieve such a significant level of peace after the war.

"What Would Jesus Do?"

One of the most awe-inspiring examples of societal change began with a fictional story. But that fictional story had an incredible real-life impact on society. *In His Steps*, a book written in 1896 by Charles Sheldon, has sold over 50 million copies and ranks as one of the best-selling books of all time.

The story takes place in a fictional town called Raymond where there is a fictional First Church, pastored by Reverend Henry Maxwell. A visitor to the church motivates Reverend Maxwell to redefine his ministry. Maxwell invites his members to make no major decisions without first asking themselves, "What would Jesus do if he were in my situation?" Several church members take on the challenge and the city of Raymond begins to transform. By the end of the book, what is happening in Raymond garners the attention of folks in Chicago, and the movement begins to grow there as well.

Over 90 years after the story was published, a youth leader at a church in Holland, Michigan, used the book to motivate and invite her youth group to take on the same challenge—to only do what they think Jesus would do in their situation. This youth minister's challenge led to the WWJD movement which has had a huge impact in our world.

4

IF IT CAN HAPPEN THERE, IT CAN HAPPEN HERE

It seems God is in the habit of moving in powerful ways when a unified group of people become fully present to themselves, to God and to each other, and they make a point to live out their faith in the community. What if your community began to do that?

As we learned in the previous chapter, there seem to be common ingredients that spurred on and maintained these movements:

- a visible item,
- a rule for life,
- and a book.

A visible item serves as a conversation starter and a way to share the movement with others. For Zinzendorf and his Order of the Mustard Seed, the visible reminder was a ring with an inscription, "None of us lives for himself." For the "What Would Jesus Do?" movement, it was a bracelet with WWJD on it.

Another common ingredient seems to be a shared rule of life which all the group members commit to follow. This gives the group direction and intentionality. For Zinzendorf that rule was: True to Christ, Kind to People, and Take the Gospel to the Nations. For Frank Buchman (Oxford Group/Moral Rearmament), that rule was: Absolute Honesty, Absolute Purity, Absolute Selflessness, Absolute Love, and all while seeking daily contact with God. For the WWJD Movement the rule was: What would Jesus do if he were in my place?

Another ingredient for the Moravians was the printed message. *The Daily Watch Word* provided unity as the members were scattered all around the world. The WWJD movement used the book, *In His Steps*.

What if you had a visible object, such as a T-shirt or bracelet, to remind you of the commitment you've made as well as be a conversation starter?

What if you had a rule for life, such as "Be fully present to myself, to God and to others while intentionally seeking unity with other Christians and living my faith in the community"?

What if you had a book, like this one, to share the vision and to focus for 40 days on being fully present, seeking unity, and living out your faith in the community?

Sounds like the ingredients for something really good!

5

A COMMITTMENT

Just as Jesus invited the disciples follow him...

Just as Paul invited Timothy to join his team...

Just as Zinzendorf and his friends chose to follow their rules for life...

Just as William Seymour committed to minister to men, women, blacks, whites, and Latinos...

Just as the members of First Church in Raymond were invited to live life always asking, "What would Jesus do?"...

Just as members of the Oxford Group and Moral Rearmament were invited by Frank Buchman to live lives of absolute honesty, absolute purity, absolute selflessness, and absolute love...

You are being invited to make a commitment.

Will you commit to

•wear a t-shirt and/or bracelet at least once a week?

•being fully present where Jesus says He will be, by connecting to other Christians as well as connecting within your community?

•participate in forty days of study and reflections to help you be more present, more unified with other Christians, and more intentional in living your faith daily?

If you choose to make this commitment, please sign the following page and send an email to me, Pastor Mark (prmark@rlcok.org), to let me know.

MY PERSONAL COMMITMENT

I, ______________________________, commit to spending the next 40 days seeking to be fully present (to myself, to God, and to the person in front of me) in the places Jesus says He will be (in Christian unity and living out my faith daily in the community.)

I will:

•wear my t-shirt and/or bracelet at least once a week to remind me of my commitment to be fully present where Jesus says He will be and be a conversation starter with others.

•participate in the 40 days of devotions in this book to grow in my ability to be present, to seek out opportunities for unity with other Christians (denominations, ethnicities, ages, economic statuses), and intentionally live my faith daily.

Date:

6

THE JOURNEY

This devotional journey is meant to be an invitation into a lifestyle where Jesus isn't just a fringe topic of your Christian life but an integral and ever-present part. From Genesis to Revelation, you will see that God designed for us to live this way.

As you travel this journey, take the time to journal what God is teaching you. The devotions will be like a cross-training program. And just as cross-training in the gym has you work different muscle groups each day, the lessons will be in five-day cycles in which you focus on the different aspects of being fully present where Jesus says He will be.

Overview of your regimen:

Days 1,6,11,16,21,26,31&36 – Being Present to Self
Days 2,7,12,17,22,27,32&37 – Being Present to God
Days 3,8,13,18,23,28,33&38 – Being Present to Our Neighbor
Days 4,9,14,19,24,29.34&39 – Encountering God with other Christians
Days 5,10,15,20,25,30,35&40 – Encountering God in the Community

Each day explore how God is leading you to be fully present where Jesus is. I whole-heartedly believe you will experience God in a more powerful way than you have to this point in your life. Also, I believe any community where believers are making this commitment will be tangibly changed at the end of 40 days. When you complete this 40-day journey, continue to view all your Bible reading through the lens of how you can be more fully present in the places Jesus says He will be.

Begin this life-changing journey with the following self-evaluation. Then, halfway through, and again at the end, you are invited to evaluate how well you are doing at being fully present (to self, to God and to others) where Jesus says He will be.

INITIAL SELF-EVALUATION

Date:

As you begin your journey toward being fully present in the places Jesus says He will be, where do you find yourself?

(1=weak, 10=strongest)

Are you present to yourself? Are you able to regularly live in the present, sit in your emotions without escaping or medicating them, and not be stuck in worries about the past or anxiety about the future?

____

Are you able to be present to God? Do you make time for personal devotions, prayer, and Bible study? Do you hear God's voice or see reminders of His presence and activity throughout the day?

____

Are you able to be present to others? Do you spend time with other people or stick to yourself? When you are in the presence of someone, are you fully available to, and aware of, the person you are with? Or are you distracted?

____

Are you intentional in seeking connections with other Christians? Do you pray for or with other Christians? Do you have relationships with other Christians where they know what is going on in your life and you know what is going on in theirs? Do you schedule Christian community into your life?

____

Are you intentional at living your faith in your daily life? Do you notice people or walk past? Do you start conversations or stay focused on your own agenda? Do you offer to pray for people when you hear they have a need?

____

Total beginning score (0-50) ____________

Are there places where you see weaknesses or deficiencies that need to be addressed during these 40 days? (Examples—addictions, broken relationships? Need to join a small group? Start talking to people I meet during the course of my day? Other?)

Things I need to work on according to my self-evaluation:

Day 1

CREATED IN GOD'S IMAGE

Present to Self

Genesis 1:26-28 Then God said, "Let us make humankind in our image, according to our likeness; and let them have dominion over the fish of the sea, and over the birds of the air, and over the cattle, and over all the wild animals of the earth, and over every creeping thing that creeps upon the earth." So God created humankind in his image, in the image of God he created them; male and female he created them. God blessed them, and God said to them, "Be fruitful and multiply, and fill the earth and subdue it; and have dominion over the fish of the sea and over the birds of the air and over every living thing that moves upon the earth."

Reflection

The Jewish creation story was different than other creation stories. No other religion viewed God as creating humanity on purpose, in God's image, for relationship with Him, and with a purpose. We need to know who we are if we are going to be present to ourselves. We were created in love and in the image of God, to partner with Him in living out a purpose much bigger than ourselves.

Prayer

Father, remind me who I am today. I am not a mistake created by accident. I am lovingly crafted in Your image and created for a purpose. AMEN

Action Step

Take time to pray or journal about how you see yourself. Talk with God about what it means to be created on purpose, in his image, and for a purpose much bigger than you.

Notes

Day 2

WALKING WITH HIM, NOT HIDING FROM HIM

Present to God

Genesis 3:6-8 So when the woman saw that the tree was good for food, and that it was a delight to the eyes, and that the tree was to be desired to make one wise, she took of its fruit and ate; and she also gave some to her husband, who was with her, and he ate. Then the eyes of both were opened, and they knew that they were naked; and they sewed fig leaves together and made loincloths for themselves. They heard the sound of the Lord God walking in the garden at the time of the evening breeze, and the man and his wife hid themselves from the presence of the Lord God among the trees of the garden.

Reflection

When we live according to God's design, there are no barriers between us and God. The enemy wants us to think we can do better on our own, without God. Adam and Eve chose to listen to the enemy, and they discovered it didn't make things better. It made them feel ashamed and disconnected from God.

One way to be present to God is to live according to His design. If you feel disconnected from God, it is likely there is some area of your life in which you've been living according to the ways of the world rather than the ways of God.

Prayer

Father, forgive me for thinking I can run my life better by myself. Show me where I have chosen to live contrary to your ways. Give me the grace and strength to realign with Your design. AMEN

Action Step

Take time today to pray or journal about where you are experiencing a disconnect from God. Ask Him to show you where you are living according to your own way or the way of the world rather than God's way.

Notes

Day 3

ENCOUNTERING GOD IN THE STRANGER

Present to Others

Genesis 18:1-5 The Lord appeared to Abraham by the oaks of Mamre, as he sat at the entrance of his tent in the heat of the day. He looked up and saw three men standing near him. When he saw them, he ran from the tent entrance to meet them, and bowed down to the ground. He said, "My lord, if I find favor with you, do not pass by your servant. Let a little water be brought, and wash your feet, and rest yourselves under the tree. Let me bring a little bread, that you may refresh yourselves, and after that you may pass on—since you have come to your servant." So they said, "Do as you have said."

Reflection

In Abraham's culture hospitality was to be shown to any strangers passing through the area. When Abraham saw three men passing by, he intentionally invited them to stop and refresh themselves. Turns out, the messengers were God's manifest presence. Not only would Abraham have missed out on an encounter with God, he and Sarai wouldn't have heard God's promise to them of a child to come which would change their lives forever.

Do you see strangers as an inconvenience or as opportunities to encounter God?

Prayer

Father, I'm sorry for placing my priorities above Yours. May I see strangers as an opportunity to encounter You. I desire to fully enter into the reason I am on this earth. AMEN

Action Step

Ask God to open your eyes to a situation which might initially seem to be a distraction but could in reality be a potential divine encounter.

Notes

Day 4

TWO ARE BETTER THAN ONE

Encountering God with Other Believers

Ecclesiastes 4:9-12 "Two are better than one, because they have a good reward for their toil. For if they fall, one will lift up the other; but woe to one who is alone and falls and does not have another to help. Again, if two lie together, they keep warm; but how can one keep warm alone? And though one might prevail against another, two will withstand one. A threefold cord is not quickly broken."

Reflection

God didn't design us to navigate life alone. We are spiritually, emotionally, and physically vulnerable when we are alone. God designed life to be experienced in community with others. We need to be intentional to invite those who haven't been able to find community. Not to shame or judge them; but to help them realize their vulnerability when all alone.

Prayer

Father, thank you for the people you have put in my life so I don't need to walk this journey alone. Where I have tried to navigate alone, build a community around me. When I see someone going through life alone, nudge me to invite them out of isolation and into community. AMEN

Action Step

Today's action step is more than just prayer or journaling. This step is admitting you, or someone you love, need help. One of the greatest enemies to being fully present to self, God, and others is ***addiction***. If the person in your life who struggles with addiction is you, TODAY is the day to break the isolation, tell someone, make an appointment with a counselor, and go to a 12-step or Celebrate Recovery group.

If the person in your life who struggles with addiction is someone you love, share your concern and offer to walk with them into healing for their addiction.

In the notes below make a commitment to yourself, or a friend, to begin the journey of healing from addiction.

Notes

Day 5

ENCOUNTERING GOD IN YOUR COMMUNITY

Deuteronomy 4:6-8 You must observe [these statutes and ordinances] diligently, for this will show your wisdom and discernment to the peoples, who, when they hear all these statutes, will say, "Surely this great nation is a wise and discerning people!" For what other great nation has a god so near to it as the Lord our God is whenever we call to him? And what other great nation has statutes and ordinances as just as this entire law that I am setting before you today?"

Reflection

Following God's laws was meant to bless those who had committed their lives to him. However, it was meant to get the neighbor's attention as well. The people of Israel were supposed to live lives of such faith, beauty, and love that the rest of the world would want what they had.

Is your faith so private that nobody sees the goodness of God when they observe you?

Or is your life public enough for people to see and want what you have?

Prayer

Father, give me the courage to be less private and more public in the way I live my life of faith. Help me to see that my faith in not just to bless me, but to witness to others that trusting you and living according to your ways is the best way to live. AMEN

Action Step

Pray or journal today about how accessible you are to others. Are you so private that your life will never draw anyone to Jesus? Or is your life visible enough that others might see and want what you have?
In the notes section write down one thing you will do today to help others see God's goodness more clearly in your life.

Notes

Day 6

BLESSED TO BE A BLESSING

Present to Self

Genesis 12:1-3 Now the Lord said to Abram, "Go from your country and your kindred and your father's house to the land that I will show you. I will make of you a great nation, and I will bless you, and make your name great, so that you will be a blessing. I will bless those who bless you, and the one who curses you I will curse; and in you all the families of the earth shall be blessed."

Reflection

By Genesis 11, the world had concluded they could be their own gods and could make it to heaven by building the tower of Babel. God, in his grace, frustrated their plans and responded by calling Abram and Sarai (who would later become Abraham and Sarah) to be his means of blessing. Not just for their family and generation, but for the whole world, for all generations.

As descendants of Abram and Sarai, aren't we the ones through whom the whole world is to be blessed? In every generation?

Prayer

Father, as a descendant of Abraham through faith in Christ, I now realize my life is not about me and my blessings, but about You blessing people through me. Help me to not just bless my generation, but like ripples on a pond, bless many generations beyond mine. AMEN

Action Step

Take time to pray or journal about how your gifts are meant not only to bless you, but to bless others. Think about how God placed you on this planet for a purpose much bigger than yourself. Ask God to show you how one of your blessings can be used more fully, not just for you, but for someone else.

Record in the notes section how you will use one of your gifts to bless someone else today.

Notes

Day 7

GOD WAS THERE THE WHOLE TIME

Present to God

Genesis 28:12-16 And [Jacob] dreamed that there was a ladder set up on the earth, the top of it reaching to heaven; and the angels of God were ascending and descending on it. And the Lord stood beside him and said, "I am the Lord, the God of Abraham your father and the God of Isaac; the land on which you lie I will give to you and to your offspring; and your offspring shall be like the dust of the earth, and you shall spread abroad to the west and to the east and to the north and to the south; and all the families of the earth shall be blessed in you and in your offspring. Know that I am with you and will keep you wherever you go, and will bring you back to this land; for I will not leave you until I have done what I have promised you." Then Jacob woke from his sleep and said, "Surely the Lord is in this place—and I did not know it!"

Reflection

Jacob ran from the consequences of cheating his brother. But God reminded him his mistakes had not removed him from God's purpose for his life. As we scheme and work hard to manage the consequences of our own choices, we often forget that God is still with us.

Are you so busy trying to compensate for the wrong choices you've made that you don't notice God is with you, offering a better option than you could ever come up with yourself?

Prayer

Father, forgive me for scheming solutions for the consequences my actions have brought on me. I realize You know what is going on and that You have a better plan than anything I could come up with on my own. I trust in You, Father. AMEN

Action Step

Talk to God about where you are trying to fix the consequences for your actions or choices by your own efforts. Ask him to reveal to you a better way.

In the note section below, write down the area of life you need to entrust to him. Then, give it to him in prayer today.

Notes

Day 8

INTERCEDING FOR OTHERS

Present to Others

Genesis 18:16-19 "Then the men set out from there, and they looked towards Sodom; and Abraham went with them to set them on their way. The Lord said, 'Shall I hide from Abraham what I am about to do, seeing that Abraham shall become a great and mighty nation, and all the nations of the earth shall be blessed in him? No, for I have chosen him, that he may charge his children and his household after him to keep the way of the Lord by doing righteousness and justice; so that the Lord may bring about for Abraham what he has promised him."

Reflection

Because Abraham showed hospitality to the three visitors, he not only heard God's promise that he and Sarah would have a child, but he also heard the judgement that was about to happen to Sodom where his nephew Lot lived. His connection with God was not just to bless himself, but to bless those he loved. Abraham interceded for his nephew and Sodom. Though judgment came to Sodom, Lot and his family were saved.

Prayer

Father, help me to intercede for those I love. Reveal to me those in need. May I not be so busy seeking my own blessing that I am unaware of how to help those I love, especially those in dangerous situations. AMEN

Action Step

In your prayer and journaling time, if God shows you a loved one who is in need, not only pray for that loved one, but contact them and let them know you are praying for them.

In the notes below, write the name(s) of those God is leading you to intercede for today. Then, place a check mark by their name when you contact them to let them know you are praying.

Notes

Day 9

WHEN GOD'S PEOPLE ARE UNIFIED

Encountering God with Other Believers

Psalm 133 "How very good and pleasant it is when kindred live together in unity! It is like the precious oil on the head, running down upon the beard, on the beard of Aaron, running down over the collar of his robes. It is like the dew of Hermon, which falls on the mountains of Zion. For there the Lord ordained his blessing, life forevermore."

Refection

The extent of God's blessings to the world is directly proportionate to the level of his followers' unity. When we are divided, God's anointing touches some areas, leaving others untouched. But when we are united, His anointing covers every area of our life and community.

Prayer

Father, may I, to the best of my ability, be at peace and unity with everyone in my community of faith, even other churches and denominations. Change my heart toward fellow believers in Christ. I desire Your blessing to be poured out abundantly for the benefit of the whole community. AMEN

Action Step

Talk with God about where you have judgments or offenses against other Christians. Select one person, church, or denomination toward whom you have negative feelings and choose to intentionally pray for and bless them today.

In the notes section, write down who you desire to bless today.

Notes

Day 10

STOP COMPLAINING AND START BLESSING

Encountering God in the Community

Jeremiah 29:7 "But seek the welfare of the city where I have sent you into exile, and pray to the Lord on its behalf, for in its welfare you will find your welfare."

Reflection

Because of their sin, God's people were defeated and taken into captivity in Babylon. Did God want them to rebel and get take revenge on their captors? No.They were God's people, and they were told to pray for the wellbeing of the city that had taken them captive.

God's people are not in the world to be a curse, but to be a blessing.

Prayer

Father, my inclination is to curse and seek harm toward those who have harmed me, but I know that only causes me to live contrary to your identity. Show me where my perceptions are wrong and give me love and grace to be a blessing to my community, even to those I have considered enemies. AMEN

Action Step

As God shows you where your perceptions might be wrong, think of ways to be a part of the healing of your community.

In the notes below record areas of your community you have criticized or complained about. Then choose to be part of the solution rather than perpetuating the problem. To bless rather than curse.

Notes

Day 11

GOD'S TREASURED POSSESSION

Present to Self

Exodus 19:5-6 [The Lord said to Moses] Now therefore, if you obey my voice and keep my covenant, you shall be my treasured possession out of all the peoples. Indeed, the whole earth is mine, but you shall be for me a priestly kingdom and a holy nation. These are the words that you shall speak to the Israelites."

Reflection

God didn't wait until the time of the New Testament to call us a kingdom of priests representing Him in the world. He said it first when He freed the Israelites from Egypt and led them to Mount Sinai. They were to be more than just freed slaves. They were God's treasured possessions, revealing His goodness and power in the world.

God set us free to be a priestly kingdom bringing His goodness to the whole world. We are to be more than forgiven sinners saved from our bondage. We are God's treasured possession.

Do you see yourself as part of God's priestly kingdom and His treasured possession?

Prayer

Father, help me to internalize that I am more than just a problem that needs to be solved. Your Word says I am Your treasured possession, not just a freed slave or forgiven sinner. Please show me what You created me to do. I am part of your priestly kingdom and I desire to reveal your goodness and power to the world. AMEN

Action Step

As you talk with God, close your eyes, and imagine yourself sitting alongside Him, not in shame or fear, but as a valued member of His team. What is He saying to you about who He sees you to be and what He has created you to do?

In the notes section, write down how you plan to implement what God revealed to you. Today. Long-term.

Notes

Day 12

SENT TO REPRESENT HIM

Present to God

Isaiah 6:1,8 In the year that King Uzziah died, I saw the Lord sitting on a throne, high and lofty; and the hem of his robe filled the temple.Then I heard the voice of the Lord saying, "Whom shall I send, and who will go for us?" And I said, "Here am I; send me!"

Reflection

King Uzziah, the king Isaiah had served for many years, died. Often the people who worked for one king were removed (or even killed) to make place for the new administration. Isaiah lived during a time of extreme uncertainty. But as he worshipped, he had a heavenly encounter. God showed Isaiah his work was not over but was just beginning. He would not just be working for a new human king but had been commissioned to work for the King of the Universe.

When we are in times of transition or uncertainty, perhaps the place to start is not strategizing, but worship. As we give God our attention in worship, we may hear Him call us into something bigger than we ever imagined.

Prayer

Father, I enjoy spending time in Your presence in worship and in prayer. Especially as I enter times of uncertainty about what comes next. I realize now the best way to find Your direction for my life is to first listen to Your calling through worship and prayer. Here I am, Lord. Send me. AMEN

Action Step

Find a place where you may easily enter into God's presence. Maybe a chapel or sanctuary. Perhaps out in the woods. Share with God the questions you have about His purpose for your life.

Write down what you hear Him say in the "Notes" section below.

Notes

Day 13

BLESSING THOSE WHO HURT YOU

Present to Others

Genesis 50:15-21 Realizing that their father was dead, Joseph's brothers said, "What if Joseph still bears a grudge against us and pays us back in full for all the wrong that we did to him?" So they approached Joseph, saying, "Your father gave this instruction before he died, 'Say to Joseph: I beg you, forgive the crime of your brothers and the wrong they did in harming you.' Now therefore please forgive the crime of the servants of the God of your father." Joseph wept when they spoke to him. Then his brothers also wept, fell down before him, and said, "We are here as your slaves." But Joseph said to them, "Do not be afraid! Am I in the place of God? Even though you intended to do harm to me, God intended it for good, in order to preserve a numerous people, as he is doing today. So have no fear; I myself will provide for you and your little ones." In this way he reassured them, speaking kindly to them.

Reflection

Out of jealousy, Joseph's brothers threw him in a well, then sold him into slavery in Egypt. After his father Jacob died, Joseph, having become a ruler in Egypt, was in a prime position to get revenge on his brothers. Therefore, when the brothers came to plead with Joseph to forgive them, they were terrified of his response.

But Joseph realized God had used even the harmful intentions of his brothers to bring about something good. Instead of vengeance, Joseph responded with love and grace. Instead of harming them as enemies, he blessed them as his family.

Has someone hurt you and now you must choose to either seek vengeance on them or seek to bless them?

Has God placed them in your life for a purpose?

Does it change the way you respond to them when you look at what God is doing to bring good out of the situation rather than what they meant for harm?

Notes

Day 13, continued

Prayer

Father, I desire to forgive rather than show vengeance. Give me the strength to look for the good You plan to achieve rather than multiplying the pain and suffering I'm tempted to inflict. AMEN

Action Step

Ask God to show you a relationship that has not been resolved. Talk with Him about how He wants you to respond. Is it time for vengeance?

Or is it time to bless and seek the best for the one who harmed you?

In the notes section, write the name (or initials) of the person who harmed you and what they did to harm you. Talk with God about how He can use it for good rather than harm.

Do you choose forgiveness or seek vengeance?
Do you choose to allow the hurt to destroy you, or make you stronger?

Notes

Day 14

A TEAM OF INDIVIDUAL PLAYERS

Encountering God with Other Believers

2 Samuel 5:1-3 Then all the tribes of Israel came to David at Hebron, and said, "Look, we are your bone and flesh. For some time, while Saul was king over us, it was you who led out Israel and brought it in. The Lord said to you: It is you who shall be shepherd of my people Israel, you who shall be ruler over Israel." So all the elders of Israel came to the king at Hebron; and King David made a covenant with them at Hebron before the Lord, and they anointed David king over Israel.

Reflection

The Israelites had been a unified group as they traveled from Egypt, through the wilderness, and into the Promised Land. But once they arrived, they began living as individual tribes in their individual tribal allotments. During that time of division, the Israelites were vulnerable to attacks from without and within.

When Saul became king, the tribes attempted to unite. But Saul had lost his blessing from God and died in battle. The individual tribes gathered around David to make him king of a unified nation. A time of peace and prosperity followed. This could never have happened if the tribes had remained separated.

Prayer

Holy Spirit, I realize I am vulnerable in my isolation. Lead me into unity with other Christians, where I and we can be stronger, together. AMEN

Action Step

If you already have a strong Christian community, thank God for that. But if you are living as an individual, confronting the challenges of life alone, ask Him to lead you into a unified, Christian community.

In the notes section below, either thank God for the community you already have, or write down a person, place, or group where God might be leading you.

Notes

Day 15

FEED A CITY, NOT JUST YOURSELF

Encountering God in the Community

2 Kings 7:8-12 When these leprous men had come to the edge of the camp [of the enemy], they went into a tent, ate and drank, carried off silver, gold, and clothing, and went and hid them. Then they came back, entered another tent, carried off things from it, and went and hid them. Then they said to one another, "What we are doing is wrong. This is a day of good news; if we are silent and wait until the morning light, we will be found guilty; therefore let us go and tell the king's household." So they came and called to the gatekeepers of the city, and told them, "We went to the Aramean camp, but there was no one to be seen or heard there, nothing but the horses tied, the donkeys tied, and the tents as they were."

Reflection

During the siege of the city of Samaria the inhabitants were starving to death. Yet the prophet Elisha prophesied there would be plenty of food the next day. It seemed impossible, but God was at work. Outside the city, four starving lepers desperately sought aid from the enemy. But they found the enemy camp abandoned. God had caused the enemy army to flee their camp quickly. And leave all their provisions!

The four lepers could have kept all the spoils for themselves, but they didn't. The lepers, the least likely of heroes, saved the city by sharing the good news.

Is there a place in your life you have discovered God's provision to meet your need? Will you keep that provision to yourself, or will you share it to help someone else have a similar need met in their life?

Prayer

Father, I have experienced emptiness. Thank You for showing me where to get my emptiness filled. May I get in the habit of showing others where to find what they need in You rather than keeping it to myself. AMEN

Action Step

Think about where you have found a resource which has given you hope and provision when you had a need. Ask God to show you a person who needs this valuable resource so they can also find hope and get their emptiness filled.

In the notes section, write the name of someone you know who has a need you either have knowledge or resources to meet.Then make a plan to help them get that need met.

Notes

Day 16

BE WHO GOD SAYS YOU ARE

Present to Self

Judges 6:11-13 Now the angel of the Lord came and sat under the oak at Ophrah, which belonged to Joash the Abiezrite, as his son Gideon was beating out wheat in the wine press, to hide it from the Midianites. The angel of the Lord appeared to him and said to him, "The Lord is with you, you mighty warrior." Gideon answered him, "But sir, if the Lord is with us, why then has all this happened to us? And where are all his wonderful deeds that our ancestors recounted to us, saying, 'Did not the Lord bring us up from Egypt?' But now the Lord has cast us off and given us into the hand of Midian."

Reflection

Because of a lack of unity between the tribes of Israel during the period of the Judges, each tribe was extremely vulnerable. Manasseh, Gideon's tribe, was being terrorized by the Midianites, and Gideon was even afraid to thresh wheat in the open, worrying it would be stolen. The angel of the Lord appeared to this frightened, insecure man and told Gideon God sees him as a mighty warrior who will deliver his tribe.

But Gideon saw himself as anything but a mighty warrior. Did he remain in fear, or did he risk becoming who God saw him to be?

Prayer

Father, help me to live according to who You called me to be. Give me strength to ignore my circumstances and past failures and no longer allow them to define my life. I leave it all in Your hands. AMEN

Action Step

First, list below all the things you are concerned about and give them to God. Second, ask God who He sees you to be. If He gives you a name or a description (such as "mighty warrior"), write it down in the notes below and ask one thing you can do today to start living that identity.

Notes

Day 17

NOT TOO BIG FOR GOD

Present to God

2 Kings 19:14-15,19 Hezekiah received the letter from the hand of the messengers and read it; then Hezekiah went up to the house of the Lord and spread it before the Lord. And Hezekiah prayed before the Lord, and said: "O Lord the God of Israel, who are enthroned above the cherubim, you are God, you alone, of all the kingdoms of the earth; you have made heaven and earth...So now, O Lord our God, save us, I pray you, from his hand, so that all the kingdoms of the earth may know that you, O Lord, are God alone."

Reflection

Assyria had systematically defeated all the nations surrounding Judah, including the northern kingdom of Israel. The emissaries of the Assyrian king, Sennacherib, were standing at the gate of Jerusalem taunting those in the city in their own language. There seemed to be no chance for Jerusalem to win against this mighty foe.

So, Hezekiah laid the letter of threat out before God. Soon after his prayer, the prophet Isaiah reported God heard their prayer and would protect them. God turned the Assyrian army against itself, and the threat went away. All other nations who had fought against Assyria had been defeated.

But the one nation which trusted God survived.

Prayer

Father, I have enemies in my life which I can't defeat by my efforts or willpower alone. I trust You to do for me what I can't do for myself. AMEN

Action Step

A recurring theme in these devotions will be addressing addiction. Few things damage our ability to be present (to ourselves, God, or others) more than addiction. Ask God to show you if there is a habit, or a substance, which is keeping you from being present (to yourself, God, and others). If something comes to mind, tell someone about it. Break the secrecy. Then commit to meet with a counselor familiar with addiction and attend a 12-step group or Celebrate Recovery. If on Day 4 you already committed to address your addiction, talk with God about how that is going. (Note – if the one who is addicted is not you but someone you love, stop condemning them for not being able to conquer it alone and commit to support and walk with them toward their freedom).

Notes

BEING THERE FOR YOUR FAMILY

Present to Others

Ruth 1:15-18 " So [Naomi] said, "See, your sister-in-law has gone back to her people and to her gods; return after your sister-in-law." But Ruth said, "Do not press me to leave you or to turn back from following you! Where you go, I will go; Where you lodge, I will lodge; your people shall be my people, and your God my God. Where you die, I will die— there will I be buried. May the Lord do thus and so to me, and more as well, if even death parts me from you!" When Naomi saw that she was determined to go with her, she said no more to her."

Reflection

Our closest neighbors are our family. Naomi left Israel with her husband and two sons to escape a famine. While in Moab her sons married. But soon her husband and both sons died. Devastated, Naomi prepared to return to Israel, sure her daughters-in-law, Ruth and Orpah, would stay in Moab and be cared for by their relatives.

But Ruth was committed to Naomi, and she refused to leave Naomi's side. Ruth's choice soon blessed her and Naomi and led her to be part of the genealogy of King David and eventually, Jesus.

Are you willing to remain faithful to your family in hard times rather than just looking out for yourself?

Prayer

Father, thank you for my family. I desire to increase my commitment to being an agent of blessing in my family. Forgive me for the times I have abandoned them or failed to love them as You called me to love them. AMEN

Action Step

Talk with God about your family. Ask Him to show you where you have not been present for them in the way He called you to be.

Who needs more of your time, more of your blessing, or more of your investment?

Who is He calling you to reconcile with?

Write any names and/or actions you are prompted to take in the notes below.

Notes

Day 19

HEALING THE HURT OF THE PAST

Encountering God with Other Believers

2 Kings 12:14-16 ...and [Rehoboam] spoke to them according to the advice of the young men, "My father made your yoke heavy, but I will add to your yoke; my father disciplined you with whips, but I will discipline you with scorpions." So the king did not listen to the people, because it was a turn of affairs brought about by the Lord that he might fulfill his word, which the Lord had spoken by Ahijah the Shilonite to Jeroboam son of Nebat. When all Israel saw that the king would not listen to them, the people answered the king, "What share do we have in David? We have no inheritance in the son of Jesse. To your tents, O Israel! Look now to your own house, O David." So Israel went away to their tents.

Reflection

It took only two generations following David's kingship for the unity he brought to Israel to fracture. David's son, Solomon, began inviting idolatry into the land. At the same time, he was using his own people for the hard work of completing his building projects. When Solomon died, the people of the ten northern tribes asked his son Rehoboam to be kinder to them than Solomon had been. And they promised they would follow him faithfully.

Instead, Rehoboam treated them even harsher, completing the fracture begun under his father. The ten tribes walked away and formed the northern kingdom of Israel, leaving Rehoboam with two tribes in the new southern kingdom of Judah. This divided kingdom lost much of its faithfulness to the God of Israel.

How might things have been different if Rehoboam had chosen mercy rather than power?

Prayer

Father, forgive me for the times I have perpetuated pre-existing hurts rather than bringing healing and mercy. Show me where unresolved hurt is weakening any of my relationships. May I be an agent of unity and reconciliation rather than the cause of division. AMEN

Action Step

Talk with God about hurt and brokenness in your closest relationships. How can you can be an agent of healing those hurts? If God brings a specific person or situation to mind, write it in the notes below.

Notes

Day 20

BRING GOOD NEWS TO OTHERS

Encountering God in the Community

Isaiah 61:1-4 The spirit of the Lord God is upon me, because the Lord has anointed me; he has sent me to bring good news to the oppressed, to bind up the brokenhearted, to proclaim liberty to the captives, and release to the prisoners; to proclaim the year of the Lord's favor, and the day of vengeance of our God; to comfort all who mourn; to provide for those who mourn in Zion— to give them a garland instead of ashes, the oil of gladness instead of mourning, the mantle of praise instead of a faint spirit. They will be called oaks of righteousness, the planting of the Lord, to display his glory. They shall build up the ancient ruins, they shall raise up the former devastations; they shall repair the ruined cities, the devastations of many generations.

Reflection

The people of Israel had experienced their full share of suffering and brokenness due to their sins. But God said the day was coming when the Spirit of the Lord would come upon His people to not only restore them but to bring hope to their neighbors and restoration to their communities. When Jesus read this scripture in the synagogue in Nazareth, it showed his mission was not to get people out of the world, but to fill them with the Holy Spirit and send them into the world as agents of healing and rebuilding.

Does knowing your relationship with God is not just for you to be blessed, but to empower you to be an agent of healing and restoration in your community change the way you live?

Prayer

Holy Spirit, fill me with all the gifts you want me to have so that I can share good news with others. Empower me to spread your message of healing and freedom and become a rebuilder of society. AMEN

Action Step

Talk to God about the gifts He has already given you and how you can use them fully.

In the notes section below, list one spiritual gift God has given you and how you can use it to help heal a situation or a build up someone you know.

Notes

HALFTIME EVALUATION

Date___________

You are halfway through your journey toward being fully present in the places Jesus says he will be. Give yourself a score on where you are in each of the following areas.

(10=Excellent...5=I've made some progress...1=Need much improvement, etc.)

______ Are you being present to yourself? Are you able to regularly live in the present, feeling your emotions without escaping or medicating them, and not be stuck in worries about the past or anxiety about the future?

______Are you being present to God? Do you make time for personal devotions, prayer, and Bible study? Do you hear God's voice or see reminders of his presence throughout the day?

______ Are you being present to others? Do you spend time with other people or isolate yourself? When you are in the presence of someone, are you fully available to, and aware of, the person you are with; or are you distracted?

______ Are you intentional in seeking unity with other Christians? Do you pray for or with other Christians? Do you have relationships with other Christians where they know what is going on in your life and you know what is going on in theirs they know what is going on in yours? Do you schedule Christian community into your life?

______Are you intentional about living out your faith in your day-to-day life? Do you stop when you notice a person in need, or walk past? Do you start conversations, or do you stay focused on your own agenda? Do you offer to pray for people when you hear they have a need?

______ Total Halftime Score (0-50)

Have you progressed with the goals you had at the beginning?

Do you have some ongoing or new goals?

Day 21

I AM NOT THE MESSIAH, I JUST POINT TO HIM

Present to Self

John 1:25-29 They asked [John the Baptist], "Why then are you baptizing if you are neither the Messiah, nor Elijah, nor the prophet?" John answered them, "I baptize with water. Among you stands one whom you do not know, the one who is coming after me; I am not worthy to untie the thong of his sandal." This took place in Bethany across the Jordan where John was baptizing. The next day he saw Jesus coming toward him and declared, "Here is the Lamb of God who takes away the sin of the world!

Reflection

John the Baptist knew who he was and who he wasn't. He didn't seek to build a community of his own followers but a community of those who would follow the One coming after him. Once he knew who Jesus was, he directed his own disciples to follow Jesus instead of remaining with him.

Knowing we are not the savior of the world can help us focus on building Jesus' kingdom instead of our own.

Prayer

Jesus, forgive me for the times I seek to draw the attention to myself rather than to You. Forgive me for trying to be "the savior of the world". May I see clearly who You are, so I am quick to direct people away from myself and toward you. AMEN

Action Step

Have a frank conversation with Jesus today about the polarity of your life.

Are you seeking followers and fans to fill your emptiness and make you feel better about yourself?

Or are you pointing others to Jesus so they can experience Him?

In the notes section below, commit to make your life about building His kingdom, not yours.

Notes

Day 22

DOING WHAT GOD IS DOING

Present to God

John 5:19 Jesus said to them, 'Very truly, I tell you, the Son can do nothing on his own, but only what he sees the Father doing; for whatever the Father does, the Son does likewise.'

Reflection

Jesus made a point to watch for what the Father was doing and then join in.

Do you live your life doing things for God, thinking He watches from a distance?

Or do you not even think about God throughout the day?

Do you expect to see Him already at work every day? And if so, do you join Him in what He is doing?

Prayer

Father, I am a disciple of Jesus, and I will do what He does. Direct my attention to see situations where You are already working. I commit to join You in that work. AMEN

Action Step

Be prepared to change your agenda as God draws your attention to people or situations you would normally pass by. Instead, stop and join the Father in the work He is doing.

Note below where you noticed God getting your attention today. What happened when you joined Him in the work He was doing?

Notes

START A CONVERSATION

Present to Others

John 4:4-7 But [Jesus] had to go through Samaria. So he came to a Samaritan city called Sychar, near the plot of ground that Jacob had given to his son Joseph. Jacob's well was there, and Jesus, tired out by his journey, was sitting by the well. It was about noon. A Samaritan woman came to draw water, and Jesus said to her, "Give me a drink."

Reflection

The story begins with Jesus and his disciples travelling from Judea to Galilee. Any "good" Jew would have walked around Samaria to avoid the hated Samaritans.But Jesus knew what the Father was up to that day in Samaria, therefore, he "had to go through Samaria." Once there, He began a conversation with a woman. He knew this was the appointment the Father had prepared for Him. Their conversation ultimately transformed the woman and her entire community. All because Jesus was in the habit of going where the Father led Him, and speaking to the person the Father put in front of Him.

Might you be one conversation away from changing the life of an individual, a family, or even an entire community?

Prayer

Father, prepare a divine appointment for me today. Show me a person with whom to start a conversation. Show me how I can pray for them or bless them. Use my availability to change someone's day and maybe even their whole life. AMEN

Action Step

Did you experience a divine appointment today? Did you allow God to lead you into a conversation?

Write about what you experienced below.

Notes

LET JESUS CHOOSE THE TEAM

Encountering God with Other Believers

Mark 3:13-19 [Jesus] went up the mountain and called to him those whom he wanted, and they came to him. And he appointed twelve, whom he also named apostles, to be with him, and to be sent out to proclaim the message, and to have authority to cast out demons. So he appointed the twelve: Simon (to whom he gave the name Peter); James son of Zebedee and John the brother of James (to whom he gave the name Boanerges, that is, Sons of Thunder); and Andrew, and Philip, and Bartholomew, and Matthew, and Thomas, and James son of Alphaeus, and Thaddaeus, and Simon the Cananaean, and Judas Iscariot, who betrayed him.

Reflection

Jesus chose "those he wanted" for his team. But the team He chose normally would not have wanted to be with each other. There were fishermen who struggled with oppressive taxes alongside a tax collector who collected those taxes. That tax collector worked for Rome, and on this same team was a Zealot, someone who delighted in killing sympathizers of the Roman government.

Jesus knew his team needed to be diverse to connect with a diverse world. In this way, He taught us that in God's kingdom, even though we're all different, all believers need to be on the same team.

Prayer

Jesus, heal my heart today. Show me where my prejudices prevent me from loving and valuing others. Help me focus more on Your will than on wanting to choose who I want on the team. AMEN

Action Step

Are there individual Christians, or groups of Christians, you have trouble loving or respecting?

Is there one person or group you believe God wants you to change your heart toward?

Make a note below who God is drawing to your attention. Then jot down a blessing you will pray for them.

Notes

Day 25

NEEDED: COMPASSIONATE WORKERS

Encountering God in the Community

Matthew 5:35-38 Then Jesus went about all the cities and villages, teaching in their synagogues, and proclaiming the good news of the kingdom, and curing every disease and every sickness. When he saw the crowds, he had compassion for them, because they were harassed and helpless, like sheep without a shepherd. Then he said to his disciples, "The harvest is plentiful, but the laborers are few; therefore ask the Lord of the harvest to send out laborers into his harvest."

Reflection

Jesus encountered the crowds in the community and had compassion on them. Jesus saw the world not as a hopeless mess, deserving judgement, but as a field, ripe and ready to experience God. He desired to meet them in their weakness and sickness and bring them into his kingdom. It was now time for the disciples to stop simply watching and start doing. It was time for them to go out to harvest.

The kingdom of God is not designed for a few special people to do ministry while others watch. It is to be a place where everyone has enough compassion to love and serve their neighbors and bring them to a relationship with God through Jesus.

Prayer

Father, when I see the needs around me, help me respond with compassion. I desire to see people who are suffering, not as problems to solve, but as individuals who need to be loved. May I see people through the lens of Your love rather than the lens of a broken world. AMEN

Action Step

When you see the brokenness of the world around you, are you overwhelmed or are you full of compassion?

Do you see people who are lost or people who are ready to be found?

Do you see their suffering as a barrier preventing them from experiencing God or as the entryway for God to reveal himself to them?

Ask God to give you His heart of compassion and His eyes of redemption and restoration.

Notes

WHEN I AM WEAK, I AM STRONG

Present to Self

2 Corinthians 12:7-10 ...even considering the exceptional character of the revelations. Therefore, to keep me from being too elated, a thorn was given to me in the flesh, a messenger of Satan to torment me, to keep me from being too elated. Three times I appealed to the Lord about this, that it would leave me, but he said to me, 'My grace is sufficient for you, for power is made perfect in weakness.' So, I will boast all the more gladly of my weaknesses, so that the power of Christ may dwell in me. Therefore I am content with weaknesses, insults, hardships, persecutions, and calamities for the sake of Christ; for whenever I am weak, then I am strong.

Reflection

During our "mountaintop experiences", we are not as likely to see God working in and through us as clearly as when we travel through the often deep valleys of life. Paul could have bragged about his amazing personal encounters with God, but he realized the fruitfulness of his life was dependent on trusting God during his times of weakness.

Have you had amazing "mountaintop" faith events?

Have you encountered dark, challenging valleys during your life? Did God reveal different things about Himself to you in the valleys than on the mountaintops?

In which of these experiences did your faith grow deeper and richer?

Prayer

Father, thank you for the mountaintop experiences You've given me. I know You work daily in and through my weakness to do what I could never do on my own. I want more than just a honeymoon with you. I want a lifetime of getting to know you for better or worse, for richer or poorer, in sickness and in health, with a relationship which even death can't part. AMEN

Action Step

Reminisce with God today about your relationship with Him.

Recall times of weakness and hopelessness through which you would have never made it without Him.

Remember how He revealed Himself to you during those events.

Jot down one example of how God has worked for you, and through you, during a time of struggle and weakness.

Notes

Day 27

IN GLORY AND SUFFERING

Present to God

Philippians 3:4,7-10 ...even though I, too, have reason for confidence in the flesh. If anyone else has reason to be confident in the flesh, I have more...Yet whatever gains I had, these I have come to regard as loss because of Christ. More than that, I regard everything as loss because of the surpassing value of knowing Christ Jesus my Lord. For his sake I have suffered the loss of all things, and I regard them as rubbish, in order that I may gain Christ and be found in him, not having a righteousness of my own that comes from the law, but one that comes through faith in Christ, the righteousness from God based on faith. I want to know Christ and the power of his resurrection and the sharing of his sufferings by becoming like him in his death.

Reflection

When we build our life on our own accomplishments, we settle for so much less than what Jesus has for us. Paul said to the Philippians that if it were a contest about having the best resume', he would win hands down. But after he met Jesus, he viewed his human accomplishments as garbage compared to his relationship with Jesus. Knowing his human weakness, Paul realized that he was nothing without Christ. From that point on, he resolved to make the rest of his life's resume' to be what Jesus did in and through him and not what he did for Jesus.

Prayer

Jesus, I let go of my human resume'. I want You to build your resume' in and through me. Reveal your glory through the power of the Holy Spirit as we walk together. Soften my heart as I travel with You into the pain and brokenness of the world. AMEN

Action Step

Make a commitment today (if you are willing) to set aside your human agenda and seek to know His will for your life.

Notes

Day 28

SALT AND LIGHT

Present to Others

Matthew 5:13-16 "You are the salt of the earth; but if salt has lost its taste, how can its saltiness be restored? It is no longer good for anything, but is thrown out and trampled underfoot. "You are the light of the world. A city built on a hill cannot be hidden. No one after lighting a lamp puts it under the bushel basket, but on the lampstand, and it gives light to all in the house. In the same way, let your light shine before others, so that they may see your good works and give glory to your Father in heaven.

Reflection

In what we call "The Sermon on the Mount" Jesus gave a picture of what His kingdom is to look like. While talking to the broken and marginalized He did more than help them feel better. He told them who they were called to be. They were not simply to have God shine His light in their darkness; they were to be the light for others.

Often, we understand our Christian faith to just be for us; our comfort, our healing, and our encouragement. But Jesus wants our focus to not be what we receive for ourselves but who we become for the sake of our neighbors.

Prayer

Father, forgive me for making my life all about my healing, my comfort and my blessings. I realize Your blessings to me are meant to bless others. May I truly be salt and light for others. AMEN

Action Step

In the notes section below, define the properties of salt and its purpose. How does that apply to the life of a Christian?

If you are to show God's light to the world, list a person you are specifically equipped to help because of your own life experience (other addicts, other divorcees...)

Notes

Day 29

DIFFERENT THAN THE REST OF THE WORLD

Encountering God with Other Believers

Matthew 5:43-47 "You have heard that it was said, 'You shall love your neighbor and hate your enemy.' But I say to you, Love your enemies and pray for those who persecute you, so that you may be children of your Father in heaven; for he makes his sun rise on the evil and on the good, and sends rain on the righteous and on the unrighteous. For if you love those who love you, what reward do you have? Do not even the tax collectors do the same? And if you greet only your brothers and sisters, what more are you doing than others? Do not even the Gentiles do the same?"

Reflection

So much of what we call unity is simply treating others well as long as we benefit from them somehow. In other words, if you are nice to me, I will reciprocate and be nice to you. But as soon I stop benefiting from having you in my life, my attitude quickly changes.

Jesus spoke of how even the Gentiles loved the people who loved them in return. He preached how we could show the world we were children of God by our love for others and what we had to offer, not by what we received in return.

What would it look like to create unity based on what we can give others rather than on what we can take from others?

Prayer

Father, give me the love and courage to relate to people as You do. And may I not just love people who are easy to love, but also those I normally consider hard to love. AMEN

Action Step

How does our heavenly Father relate to people? What are some of your traits that need to change so you can relate to others as a child of God?

Make a short list of His attributes that you can emulate to be more like Him.

Notes

AS WE GO

Encountering God in the Community

Luke 8:42-44 As [Jesus] went, the crowds pressed in on him. Now there was a woman who had been suffering from hemorrhages for twelve years; and though she had spent all she had on physicians, no one could cure her. She came up behind him and touched the fringe of his clothes, and immediately her hemorrhage stopped.

Reflection

Much of the biblical record of Jesus' ministry takes place as He and His disciples journeyed from one place to another. In Luke 8, Jesus had just been asked by Jairus, a leader of the synagogue, to come and heal his sick, 12-year-old daughter. Only because He was out in public and accessible was Jairus able to invite Him. God even worked through Him to heal a woman on the way to Jairus' house!

By the time Jesus walks to Jairus' home, Jairus' daughter has died. Through God's power and compassion, Jesus brings her back to life. None of the miracles that day would have happened if Jesus had just sat in his "ministry office," unavailable to the public. He spent most of His time out in the community, loving and blessing the people He came to save.

Prayer

Father, I realize I miss out blessing others because I'm not regularly out in the community. Create a divine appointment for me today with someone who needs to be blessed. Help me to be where people like Jairus and the woman who touched Jesus' garment can connect with me, and I can supply a healing word or touch. AMEN

Action Step

Leave your home or office for a while today to be where people have access to you.

Below, list a couple of places you might visit where you will be more accessible to someone in need of a compassionate word or blessing.

Notes

Day 31

KNOWING WHO YOU ARE

Present to Self

2 Timothy 1:11-12 For this gospel I was appointed a herald and an apostle and a teacher, and for this reason I suffer as I do. But I am not ashamed, for I know the one in whom I have put my trust, and I am sure that he is able to guard until that day what I have entrusted to him.

Reflection

Paul encouraged Timothy to be faithful to God's calling on his life. Paul knew he was a herald, an apostle, and a teacher of the gospel. And because he knew his purpose, he was willing to suffer to be faithful to that calling. He trusted God to be there for him ***as*** he lived out his calling.

When you know what you are called for, it is much easier to stay committed and to do whatever is necessary to be faithful to that calling.

Prayer

Father, reveal me who I am and why I am alive. I want to be faithful to Your calling. Remind me that You are with me as I live out my purpose day by day. And give me the courage and love to do whatever it takes to carry out Your will for my life. AMEN

Action Step

Have a conversation with God about why you are alive.
What is the primary calling God has on your life?
Who has God placed in your life to be committed to, for better or worse?
Are you committed to living out God's purpose for you?
Are you willing to fulfill your calling to God and your commitment to the people God has put in your life?

In the notes below, write out your answers to these important questions.

Notes

Day 32

PRESENT YOURSELF TO GOD

Present to God

Romans 6:13-16 No longer present your members to sin as instruments of wickedness but present yourselves to God as those who have been brought from death to life and present your members to God as instruments of righteousness. For sin will have no dominion over you since you are not under law but under grace. What then? Should we sin because we are not under law but under grace? By no means! Do you not know that if you present yourselves to anyone as obedient slaves, you are slaves of the one whom you obey, either of sin, which leads to death, or of obedience, which leads to righteousness?

Reflection

When we have received Jesus, our sins no longer determine our destination. But they do affect our present experiences and relationships with God and those around us. We may think we have presented our sins to God for forgiveness so everything will be fine. But God doesn't just ask us to present our sins to Him for our sake—He desires us to present ourselves to Him for the sake of the world.

What would my wife think if all I offered her were bills to pay, but never let her share in our bank account, my life, my time, my energy, and my love? Yes, we are assured a destination in heaven if we present our sins to God. But we will only experience the activity of heaven in this life if we present our heart, soul, mind, and strength to Him, right now, between here and heaven.

Prayer

Jesus, I brought my sins to Your cross for forgiveness. Now I submit myself to You, for what you want to do in and through me for your kingdom. Today, I give you not just my sins, but also my heart, soul, mind, and strength. AMEN

Action Step

Take some time to ask yourself some hard questions.

What are you really offering God in your day-to-day life?

Are you offering a wish list of what you want from Him, or are you offering your life to be used by Him?

Did you ask your sins to be forgiven just for your sake, or to free you to love and live for the sake of others?

Fill in the two lists below, then talk with God about what those columns say about your relationship with Him.

Notes

Give to/take from God to love myself	***Give to/receive from God to love others***

Day 33

OUT OF SIGHT, BUT NOT OUT OF MIND

Present to Others

1 Timothy 4:12-15 Let no one despise your youth but set the believers an example in speech and conduct, in love, in faith, in purity. Until I arrive, give attention to the public reading of scripture, to exhorting, to teaching. Do not neglect the gift that is in you, which was given to you through prophecy with the laying on of hands by the council of elders. Put these things into practice, devote yourself to them, so that all may see your progress.

Reflection

From the time Paul first met Timothy in Lystra, he recognized the calling of God on Timothy's life. In this scripture, Timothy has gotten tired and discouraged and Paul has written to remind him of God's calling, so he doesn't give up. Because of his young age, Timothy was not respected as a minister. But Paul reminded Timothy of the gifts in him from God and imparted to him by the elders.

Because they were in different cities, Timothy was out of Paul's sight and often far from his mind. But Paul sought to be present to Timothy through a letter since he couldn't be there in person.

Are there people in your life who are out of sight and out of your thoughts?

Do you need to let them know they are still in your heart and mind even though they reside elsewhere?

Prayer

Father, bring to my mind someone in my life, near or far, who needs to be encouraged and strengthened. Use me to help them fulfill the purposes You have for their life.. AMEN

Action Step

Take time to make a call, send a letter, text, or email to someone you haven't seen for a while. Or make plans to visit them in person, to encourage and bless them. If God brings them to your mind, there is a reason for it.

In the notes below, write down someone God brings to your mind and how you will connect with them, bless them, and encourage them.

Notes

Day 34

MAINTAINING UNITY OF THE SPIRIT

Encountering God with Other Believers

Ephesians 4:1-6 I therefore, the prisoner in the Lord, beg you to lead a life worthy of the calling to which you have been called, with all humility and gentleness, with patience, bearing with one another in love, making every effort to maintain the unity of the Spirit in the bond of peace. There is one body and one Spirit, just as you were called to the one hope of your calling, one Lord, one faith, one baptism, one God and Father of all, who is above all and through all and in all.

Reflection

Paul taught the Ephesians about spiritual gifts. But he emphasized being good stewards of those gifts. He instructed them to live in unity with each other and use those spiritual gifts to build up others, not just themselves. God's prerequisite for having and using spiritual gifts includes treating each other with humility, gentleness, and patience.

Could it be God is not anointing you with spiritual gifts because He knows your goal is not to use those gifts to love and serve others?

Prayer

Father, I desire to have Your spiritual gifts. Prepare and motivate me to use them for the right purpose. Mold me into a person of humility, gentleness, patience, and love who realizes Your gifts are for the sake of building up others, not just myself. AMEN

Action Step

Ask God if your heart and character are ready for Him to bestow spiritual gifts to you. Ask Him what shortcomings you need to work on so you may be a good steward of His gifts.

In the notes section, jot down changes to your heart and character you desire to make to be more available to God and to your neighbor.

Notes

Day 35

FREEDOM TO SERVE

Encountering God in the Community

Galatians 5:13-15 For you were called to freedom, brothers and sisters; only do not use your freedom as an opportunity for self-indulgence, but through love become slaves to one another. For the whole law is summed up in a single commandment, 'You shall love your neighbor as yourself.' If, however, you bite and devour one another, take care that you are not consumed by one another.

Reflection

The freedom we have in Christ is meant to guide us in love towards our neighbor. If our freedom is used to simply bless ourselves, we will experience very little of God's kingdom in our lives. We begin experiencing God's presence on a regular basis when our freedom is used to love, serve, and bless our neighbor.

Prayer

Father, thank you for setting me free. I pray to use my freedom to love and serve others so I may fully experience and spend time with You between now and the time I die. AMEN

Action Step

Ask God to show you how to really bless someone else today.

Maybe bringing flowers, paying for someone's dinner, mowing someone's lawn, etc.

Practice spending time in God's presence by blessing others.

Make a note below of something God shows you to do to truly bless someone else.

Notes

Day 36

YOU'RE STILL ON THE TEAM

Present to Self

John 21:15-17 When they had finished breakfast, Jesus said to Simon Peter, "Simon son of John, do you love me more than these?" He said to him, "Yes, Lord; you know that I love you." Jesus said to him, "Feed my lambs." A second time he said to him, "Simon son of John, do you love me?" He said to him, "Yes, Lord; you know that I love you." Jesus said to him, "Tend my sheep." He said to him the third time, "Simon son of John, do you love me?" Peter felt hurt because he said to him the third time, "Do you love me?" And he said to him, "Lord, you know everything; you know that I love you." Jesus said to him, "Feed my sheep."

Reflection

Peter told Jesus he would never deny him. So, he really messed up when he denied he knew Jesus three times. He had even made eye contact with Jesus during his third denial. There was no way Jesus would want him on his team again.

Or so Peter thought.

The angel at the tomb told the women to tell the disciples "and Peter" that he would meet them in Galilee. Jesus had not given up on him! In Galilee, Jesus prepared a breakfast and enabled Peter to have another miraculous catch of fish—just like the day he was first called. Jesus knew Peter's heart, and He had no intention of cutting Peter from His team. Jesus set up this entire event to restore Peter.

Have you messed up in the past and feel disqualified from being on Jesus' team? Jesus is seeking to meet you today to assure you that you are still on His team. He is in the business of restoring, not canceling. Canceling is what satan does. But Jesus pursues you to restore you to your purpose.

Prayer

Jesus, I want to serve you. See my heart today, not my past failures. Seat me at your table and remind me I am still on your team. Turn my attention from the mistakes of my past and towards Your purpose for my present and future. AMEN

Action Step

Sit with Jesus today and let him heal your heart and restore you to your purpose.

In the note section, list the reasons you think you deserve to be kicked off his team. Then listen as He responds to your failures with words of forgiveness and restoration.

Notes

Day 37

TREASURE IN EARTHEN VESSELS

Present to God

2 Corinthians 4:5-7 For we do not proclaim ourselves; we proclaim Jesus Christ as Lord and ourselves as your slaves for Jesus' sake. For it is the God who said, "Let light shine out of darkness," who has shone in our hearts to give the light of the knowledge of the glory of God in the face of Jesus Christ. But we have this treasure in clay jars, so that it may be made clear that this extraordinary power belongs to God and does not come from us.

Reflection

Our weakness does not disqualify us from access to God's presence. It is in our weakness that God chooses to dwell. God living within us is what draws people to us. We can't accomplish what God has called us to do by ourselves. He takes our brokenness and weakness and reveals Himself through us, in our jars of clay, His earthen vessels.

Prayer

Holy Spirit, help me to stop trying to earn my access to God through my own strength, and to realize You desire to dwell in me just the way I am. Forgive me for hiding You by pretending I have no cracks and revealing to others only myself and not You. I want to reveal my cracks and brokenness and make it clear that my strength doesn't come from me, but from the One living in me. AMEN

Action Step

Are you trying to do things for God through your own competence? Begin the day by allowing His Spirit to live in and through your weakness, showing the world God's strength and love.

In the notes, write down an area of brokenness and vulnerability that causes you to hide from God. Then invite Him to fully inhabit that area of your life and give someone else a glimpse of God through that weakness.

Notes

Day 38

Being Who Your Neighbor Needs

Present to Others

Psalm 41:9 - 9Even my bosom friend in whom I trusted, who ate of my bread, has lifted the heel against me.

Reflection

It is one thing to be hurt by an enemy, but it is entirely different when a friend hurts you. King David was surrounded by enemies who sought to kill him. But his greatest pain occurred when he was betrayed by those who claimed to be friends.

Jesus quoted this Psalm in John 13, referring to Judas, one of his friends, who betrayed him. It is often those who are closest to us that cause us the most pain and trauma. Often they are not who we expect or need them to be.

Have you claimed to be a friend but instead inflicted trauma rather than blessing? It's time to be present and heal relationships you have hurt or abandoned!

Prayer

Father, reveal to me where I have inflicted harm and trauma upon a friend rather than blessing. Give me strength to heal our relationship so that I can once again be a blessing rather than a curse. AMEN

Action Step

Ask God to reveal to you places where you have caused more harm than blessing to a friend. If a name or names come up, ask God how to make amends and restore your friendship to one of blessing rather than harm.

Write the names and actions below.

Notes

Day 39

WHY DO WE NEED CHRISTIAN UNITY?

Encountering God with Other Believers

James 5:14-16 Are any among you sick? They should call for the elders of the church and have them pray over them, anointing them with oil in the name of the Lord. The prayer of faith will save the sick, and the Lord will raise them up; and anyone who has committed sins will be forgiven. Therefore confess your sins to one another, and pray for one another, so that you may be healed. The prayer of the righteous is powerful and effective.

Reflection

Why do we need Christian unity? There is forgiveness and healing that will never be fully experienced when we live our lives without Christian community. Many addicts experience healing when they come out of isolation and receive love and grace in a community of faith. People suffering trauma and sickness often experience healing when they receive prayers and have hands laid on them in Christian community.

Why do many of us go to church every week, yet never allow anyone to know our suffering, let alone pray for us? Christian community is meant to be a place to experience truth, healing, love, and community as we share our lives with each other.

Prayer

Father, I don't want to live my life of faith alone. Give me Christian community where I can be fully known and fully loved. Give me fellow believers who will lay hands on me and pray for me. I want to experience and participate in the powerful love and prayers of others. AMEN

Action Step

Make a commitment to start conversations with fellow believers and make friendships where you can be known, touched, loved, and prayed for regularly. It may be joining a small group in your church, seeking to go deeper with a group you are already part of, or building your own community of Christian friends to share life with.

In the notes, make a plan to upgrade your experience of Christian community.

Notes

Day 40

THE NEED IS GREAT, THE LABORERS ARE FEW

Encountering God in the Community

Luke 10:1-9 After this the Lord appointed seventy others and sent them on ahead of him in pairs to every town and place where he himself intended to go. He said to them, "The harvest is plentiful, but the laborers are few; therefore ask the Lord of the harvest to send out laborers into his harvest. Go on your way. See, I am sending you out like lambs into the midst of wolves. Carry no purse, no bag, no sandals; and greet no one on the road. Whatever house you enter, first say, 'Peace to this house!' And if anyone is there who shares in peace, your peace will rest on that person; but if not, it will return to you. Remain in the same house, eating and drinking whatever they provide, for the laborer deserves to be paid. Do not move about from house to house. Whenever you enter a town and its people welcome you, eat what is set before you; cure the sick who are there, and say to them, 'The kingdom of God has come near to you.'

Reflection

Jesus saw the needs of the community and had compassion, so he sent out the twelve to do what He Himself had been doing. But twelve were not enough for the needs of the entire world. So, he sent out seventy to do what He had been doing.

What they had to offer a world in need was not money or supplies. They were to offer a relationship with God. They didn't set out with fancy programs or gimmicks. They simply prayed the Holy Spirit would show them where to go. And when they arrived, they ate with people, shared life with people, and prayed for people. As they traveled, people experienced love, healing, and the tangible presence of God. Individual lives and entire communities were changed.

The need is too big to be met by pastors and professional Christians only. It can only be met when all of God's people live their lives being led and empowered by the Holy Spirit, loving people, healing people, and changing the world, one relationship at a time.

Is God waiting for you to be led by the Spirit, to know who to spend time with today?

Are you willing to sit at someone's table, get to know and love them, pray for them, and tell them about Jesus?

(continued on next page)

Notes

Day 40, continued

Prayer

Jesus, send me out today. Help me to notice people to whom You are leading me and to take time to share life with them. AMEN

Action Step

Try the following process in your morning prayer time:

1. Ask God to show you where to go today.
2. Ask God to lead you to people or situations in which He is already at work.

Then, when God does lead you into divine appointments:

3. Be present to that person so you hear their stories and know their needs.
4. Pray for that person and tell them Jesus loves them.
5. Ask God if there is anything else he wants you to do and do it.

After practicing this process of being led by God into a divine encounter today, commit to God to make yourself available to such encounters every day.

Notes

FINAL SELF-EVALUATION

As you finish your 40-day journey toward being fully present in the places Jesus says He will be, evaluate where you are (from 1-10) at each of the following:

(1=weak, 10=strongest)

______How are you doing being present to yourself? Are you able to regularly live in the present, sit in your emotions without escaping or medicating them, and not be stuck in worries about the past or anxiety about the future?

______How are you doing at being present to God? Do you make time for personal devotions, prayer, and Bible study? Do you hear God's voice or see reminders of his presence and activity throughout the day?

______How well are you doing at being present to others? Do you spend time with other people or spend most of your time alone? When you are in the presence of someone, are you fully available and aware of the person you are with? Or are you distracted?

______How intentional are you in seeking unity with other Christians? Do you pray for or with other Christians? Do you have relationships with other Christians where they know what is going on in your life? Do you schedule time for Christian community into your life?

______How intentional are you at living out your faith in your day-to-day life? Do you notice people or walk past? Do you start conversations or stay focused on your own agenda? Do you offer to pray for people when you hear they have a need for prayer?

______Total Final Score (0-50)

Goals:
How are you doing with the goals you set at the beginning?

At the halfway mark?

What continuing or new goals do you have?

Have you experienced God because you set a goal of being fully present where Jesus said He would be? Please consider sharing your testimony and/or experience with me at Prmark@rlcok.org.

May your encounters with Jesus continue to multiply and be more tangible as you live life seeking to be fully present where Jesus says He will be!

Pastor Mark Borseth

If you would like to order a t-shirt (shown on Pastor Mark, next page), please scan this QR code:

Pastor Mark Borseth grew up on a farm outside Decorah, Iowa. Early on, his experiences of church were almost exclusively through the Lutheran church, but God has led him on a journey of getting to know Him better through a diverse group of friendships and experiences with other denominations and streams of the church during his 27 years of ministry.

Pastor Mark earned his Bachelor of Science in Chemistry from Winona State University (MN). After college, his involvement with Lutheran Youth Encounter (Minneapolis MN) for five years led him away from his plan to get his PhD in Chemistry and to go instead into ministry.

Borseth attended seminary training at Luther Seminary in St Paul, Minnesota and graduated with his Master of Divinity in 1997. From 2007 to 2008, Mark experienced more of the Charismatic/ Pentecostal stream of the church by attending Global School of Supernatural Ministry in Mechanicsburg, Pennsylvania.

Pastor Mark has served congregations in Beloit, Wisconsin, Minneapolis, Minnesota, Harrisburg, Pennsylvania, and Harvest, Alabama. He has served at Resurrection Lutheran Church in Yukon, Oklahoma since 2012.

Pastor Mark Borseth and his wife Betsy have three sons—Nathan, Andrew and Peter.

www.ingramcontent.com/pod-product-compliance
Lightning Source LLC
Chambersburg PA
CBHW082112120626
46553CB00011B/3648
* 9 7 9 8 9 8 9 7 1 5 4 9 7 *